THE
TARKA TRAIL

• A PAST and PRESENT COMPANION •

London and South Western Rly.

From BUDE.   787

TO

Barnstaple Town

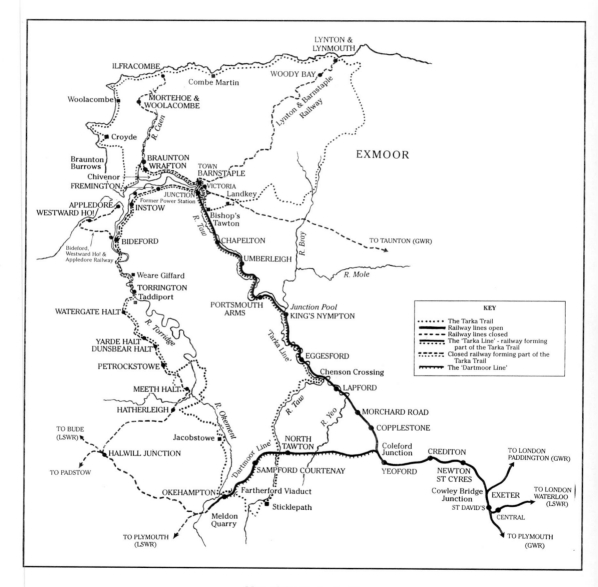

Map of the Tarka Trail.

THE
TARKA TRAIL

· A PAST and PRESENT COMPANION ·

A nostalgic journey along old railway lines by foot and cycle

Terry Gough

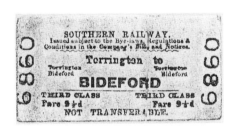

· RAILWAY HERITAGE ·
from
The NOSTALGIA Collection

First published in July 1998

British Library Cataloguing in Publication Data

A catalogue record for this book is available from the British Library.

ISBN 1 85895 140 2

Past & Present Publishing Ltd
The Trundle
Ringstead Road
Great Addington
Kettering
Northamptonshire NN14 4BW

Map drawn by Christina Siviter

Some of the material in this book first appeared in *British Railways Past and Present Special: The Tarka Trail*, published by Past & Present in 1995.

Printed and bound in Great Britain

Past and Present

A Past & Present book
from
The NOSTALGIA *Collection*

Title page **Several stations were still issuing Southern Railway tickets to local destinations in the 1960s. Petrockstowe even sold a 1st Class single on 29 July 1963 for 1s 2d, but the booking clerk, probably amazed that anyone should wish to travel 1st Class on an almost empty single-coach branch-line train, forgot to enter the destination. The spelling of Petrockstowe varied during the lifetime of the line, and some tickets omitted the last letter.** *Author's collection*

Below **A Southern Railway excursion advertisement. Note that Bideford to Hatherleigh is only available on Tuesdays despite a daily service being provided. Tuesday was (and still is) market day.**

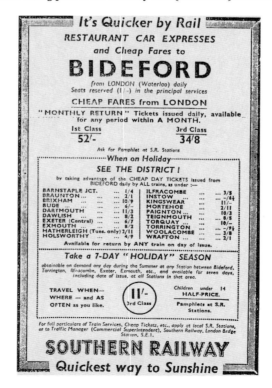

CONTENTS

Introduction and acknowledgements 7

The Tarka Trail: northern section
  Barnstaple to Lynton & Lynmouth and Ilfracombe 9
The Tarka Trail: south-western section
  Barnstaple to Bideford, Torrington and Hatherleigh 30

Bibliography 63
Index of locations 64

A plaque commemorating the opening of the Tarka Trail displayed at Bideford station. *TG*

A high-level view from the road bridge overlooking Torrington station, with plenty of milk traffic in evidence. Class '25' No 25058 undertakes some shunting on 3 September 1978.

The view today is little different, in that the main building still stands although it has taken on a new role. It is in everyday use as a public house (The Puffing Billy), which provides refreshment of very good value to the many walkers and cyclists on the Tarka Trail. Little did those responsible for the decision to convert the station into a pub realise that one day customers would arrive by 'rail' again. *Spencer Taylor/TG*

Author's collection

INTRODUCTION

The Tarka Trail is a long distance recreational route in North Devon completed in 1992, which gives visitors the opportunity to enjoy the area without the intrusion of the motor car. It is centred on Barnstaple, from which it describes a figure of eight, with its extremities at Lynton and Okehampton. Different parts of the Trail can be covered by rail, by foot and by cycle, and in total it covers 180 miles of some of the most beautiful countryside in the United Kingdom.

The various elements of the Trail are not all new and a significant part makes use of railway lines. Both Barnstaple and Okehampton can be reached by train from Exeter and part of the line to Barnstaple constitutes the Trail itself; these two lines are covered in the companion book, *The Tarka and Dartmoor Lines*.

Closed railway lines also form part of the Trail, including a section of the Barnstaple to Ilfracombe line. South-west of Barnstaple the Trail uses the line that followed the River Torridge to Bideford and Torrington. Beyond Torrington the trackbed of the North Devon & Cornwall Junction Light Railway (NDCJLR) is used almost to Hatherleigh.

Long-established public footpaths make up other parts of the Tarka Trail, for example that between Barnstaple and Lynton, which crosses the old railway line from Taunton to Barnstaple near Landkey, then climbs Exmoor to join the Two Moors Way for the walk to Lynton. The Two Moors Way, as its name implies, links Exmoor and Dartmoor and ends at Ivybridge, more than 100 miles from the North Devon coast; it passes close to Morchard Road station, on the Exeter to Barnstaple line. At Lynton the terminus of the closed narrow-gauge Lynton & Barnstaple Railway can still be seen.

Elsewhere the Trail uses minor roads, particularly where there is no public footpath and it has not proved possible to obtain permission to use privately owned land. Much of the Trail between Meeth and Okehampton falls into this category.

The part of the Trail suitable for cyclists is restricted mainly to the former railway lines, which provide an excellent way for people of all ages to enjoy the area in complete safety and without the same level of exertion necessary for other parts of the Trail. Horse riding is permitted (at least experimentally) along the former railway line from Torrington to Petrockstowe.

Much has been published on the area covered by the Trail, by far the best known being the book *Tarka the Otter* by Henry Williamson, first published in 1927, whose fictional journeys around northern Devon are traced by the Trail's route. There are also many books on local history, and those that are out of print are available in public libraries and the North Devon Record Office in Barnstaple. Some address a particular aspect (such as Chivenor Airfield), while others are of a more general nature and give more of an overview for the visitor. An example is the Warner *Red Guide*, which gives information on many of the towns and villages through which the Trail passes.

A few books discuss the railway history of North Devon, with the building of the Taw Valley Railway between Barnstaple and Fremington, the arguments over the merits of the broad and standard gauge, establishment of a network throughout North Devon, and its ultimate decline in recent years. The short life of the narrow-gauge Lynton & Barnstaple Railway is also recorded in several books. There was also a narrow-gauge mineral line in the Torrington and Petrockstowe area, which was later absorbed into one of the last railway lines to be built in the United Kingdom. This was the line from Torrington to Halwill Junction, opened in 1925.

North Devon has seen many changes since *Tarka the Otter* was written. Some of these changes have been brought about by forces external to North Devon, in particular the desire of people from the crowded parts of the United Kingdom to experience another lifestyle and environment. There is inevitably a conflict of interests, but despite the economic pressure to attract visitors to North Devon, the environment has suffered far less than other once isolated parts of the country. Industrial development has also taken place, and the coming of the canal, then the railway, did much to enhance both tourism and industry; the latter is based mostly on local resources, especially related to farming.

The decline of the railway has been brought about mainly by the ever-increasing availability of the motor vehicle and by the demands of local industry to use what was perceived as more convenient road transport. Despite the shift from rail to road by both passengers and freight, most roads in North Devon do not have a significantly greater carrying capacity than in the immediate past decades. Although Barnstaple has had a succession of peripheral routes designed to avoid the town centre, and some of the villages have bypasses, most towns and villages are still immediately recognisable from photographs taken in Henry Williamson's time. The vast majority also remain unspoilt.

Similarly with the countryside; although hosting an ever-increasing number of visitors, the much greater awareness in recent years of the need to protect and preserve our inheritance has led to an increasing respect for the environment. Hence the birth in 1989 of the Tarka Project under the auspices of Devon County Council, four district councils and the Countryside Commission, which led to the creation of the Tarka Trail.

The theme of Tarka clearly appeals to the emotions and consciences of the many people who are familiar with *Tarka the Otter*. Visitors can see that they are welcome to visit North Devon, they can contribute economically to the area, and with common sense and sensitivity enjoy the beauty without jeopardising the special nature of the environment for future generations. The Tarka Project is succeeded by the Tarka Country Tourism Association, which promotes 'green' tourism, and the Tarka Country Trust, through which visitors can make donations towards the conservation of the area.

I have visited the area many times, in my early years by bicycle as part of my annual grand tour of the South West, joined after a few years by a young lady. Later in life the holidays were spent camping between Barnstaple and Ilfracombe, admittedly travelling from home by car. Life has now turned almost full circle; the children are themselves adults and the young lady and I now come to North Devon to enjoy the Tarka Trail by bicycle, as many others do, either bringing their own or hiring bikes at one of the many outlets along the way. This book has been written as a photographic reflection on the changes that have occurred at the places once served by the railway, and which now form part of the Tarka Trail.

ACKNOWLEDGEMENTS

Most importantly I wish to record my thanks for support over so many years to the young lady on the bicycle, my wife Cynthia. She has accompanied me on all visits to obtain material for this book, in the course of which she has cycled many miles and spent hours in the North Devon Record Office searching the archives for suitable material. I thank her for her patience, support and encouragement. At the Record Office, we have received a great deal of help and advice from Bryony Harris, who also undertook the processing of all the photographs attributed to the Beaford Archive.

I gratefully acknowledge the various photographers whose names are recorded in the captions. I thank Derek Mercer for expertly printing my own material. I also thank Committee members of the Bideford & Instow Railway Group and Joy Slocombe, Curator of Ilfracombe Museum, for providing access to their archives. I am grateful for the interest shown in this edition by Devon County Council and the Tarka Project.

Terry Gough
Sherborne, Dorset

THE TARKA TRAIL: NORTHERN SECTION

The north-east segment of the Tarka Trail across the edge of Exmoor starts from Barnstaple station (formerly Barnstaple Junction station) and, once it leaves the Barnstaple area, is not suitable for cyclists, as it does not use old railways. It does, however, cross two former lines, and to that extent has a place in this book. We shall travel round this section of the 'figure eight' in an anti-clockwise direction, from Barnstaple round via Lynmouth, Lynton, Ilfracombe and Mortehoe, and back to Barnstaple.

Opened in 1874, the Barnstaple to Ilfracombe line lasted almost 100 years, being closed by BR in 1970. On 14 August 1963 the 2.20 pm Ilfracombe to Waterloo train approaches Barnstaple Junction hauled by ex-Southern Railway Bulleid 'Battle of Britain' Class 'Light Pacific' No 34069 *Hawkinge*.

Following closure there were attempts by private organisations to run the line, but these did not come to fruition. Today the embankment has been grassed and the trackbed on to Braunton, on the other side of the river, forms part of the Tarka Trail. *P. Hutchinson/TG*

Opposite Starting from Barnstaple Junction the Trail crosses the attractive bridge over the River Taw. The railway crossed at the same point, which gave good views of the trains to and from Ilfracombe. A freight train bound for Ilfracombe in the early 1960s is hauled by Class 'N' No 31846. Barnstaple Town station is just beyond the signal box on the east bank.

The railway bridge was dismantled in 1977 and the view from the road is now unimpeded. Consideration is currently being given to building a new bridge further downstream to reinstate the railway as far as Braunton. The skyline has changed and the modern three-storey buildings on the riverside are adjacent to the old Barnstaple Town station, which still exists (see page 28). The much taller building beyond is the Civic Centre, housing the offices of North Devon District Council and Devon & Cornwall Constabulary. *R. C. Riley/TG*

Right These two Knight advertisments date from 1924 and 1997 and are grandfather and grandson. Several of Mr Knight senior's photographs are reproduced in this book, including the one seen here.

Above and right At the town end of the road bridge is the North Devon Museum, and from here the Trail follows the east bank of the river, from which excellent views are obtained of the bridge. The factory of Messrs Shapland on the west bank is evident in both photographs, which were taken about 60 years apart. There is an expanding cycle route network within Barnstaple and apart from encouraging cycling for local journeys, it also serves as a convenient link between the southern and northern sections of the Tarka Trail. *R. L. Knight/TG*

While in this part of Barnstaple, it is worth a short diversion at Newport to visit the site of the GWR's Victoria station and goods yard, much of which is now buried under what is named the Great Western Industrial Estate. One of the railway buildings has, however, survived, and this is the goods shed, part of which is now a Christian church. A main road covers the railway trackbed adjacent to the platform, while the platforms themselves are mostly within a South Western Electricity depot. *R. L. Knight/TG*

The Trail joins the A377 (Exeter Road) after passing under the North Devon Link Road. At Bishop's Tawton (see *The Tarka and Dartmoor Lines*) the Trail leaves the main road and shortly thereafter becomes a footpath to Landkey. Although there is no railway station at Landkey, the GWR line from Taunton passed close to the village and the main road (Blakes Hill Road) passed through the centre of the village. There is little trace of the railway today; the trackbed lies under the North Devon Link Road, the new A361.

The main road through Landkey in the days before the village was inflicted with the continual passage of motor vehicles. The end cottage was a filling station, and on the extreme right was a general stores. The road leading from the right is Tanners Road.

   Thanks to the North Devon Link Road the village has claimed back much of the quiet of former days, as the old main road is now used mostly by local traffic. All the cottages on the right are now private residences. *Beaford Archive/TG*

After leaving the Landkey area, the Trail heads east until it reaches the River Bray; the North Devon Link Road uses the former railway viaduct to cross the river. The Trail then heads north across Exmoor and has no further interaction with railways until it reaches Lynmouth.

My first visit to Lynmouth served as a dramatic demonstration of both the beauty and destructive power of nature. This was the summer of 1952 shortly after the floods that destroyed most of the village and caused considerable loss of life. Here was a peaceful village built at the mouth of the East and West Lyn Rivers surrounded by the steep sides of the valley. With little warning this peace was literally shattered, and the character of the village permanently changed. The visitor today will still encounter beauty in the river and its surroundings, although they now look very different.

Immediately above Lynmouth is Lynton, reached by a cliff railway opened in 1890 and still providing by far the quickest and least exhausting mode of transport between the two villages. The cliff railway was financed by Sir George Newnes and built by Mr R. Jones. These two people played the same roles in relation to Lynton Town Hall (see page 16). The railway consists of two adjacent tracks on each of which is a single coach attached to a common cable. Each coach houses a tank and by filling the coach at the top of the incline with water, it becomes heavier than the one at the bottom and, as it descends, the bottom coach ascends.

The best view of the cliff railway is from the mouth of the river at Lynmouth. All the buildings shown in the early photograph still stand, although the tower (the Rhenish Tower) was destroyed during the 1952 flood and rebuilt two years later. The unusually designed corner building is now a gift shop with holiday accommodation above, while the thatched building is the Rising Sun Hotel. A new wall separating the harbour from the river was built following the flood. *Bill Pryor/TG*

14

There was another railway here, the Lynton &
Barnstaple Railway (L&BR), which was also
financed by Sir George Newnes. It was opened
in 1898 and provided both passenger and
freight facilities until complete closure in 1935.

Above The terminus of the line was situated even
higher than Lynton village. Much has been written
about this railway and it is regrettable that it was
closed long before its potential value as a tourist
attraction in its own right was recognised.

The station buildings are now in use as a private
residence and externally are almost unchanged. The
main building includes accommodation to let during
the holiday season, and the goods shed has also been
converted into residential accommodation. There are
other surviving stations on the line, particularly Woody
Bay (see page 17) and Blackmoor Gate, but the course
of the railway is far from the Tarka Trail. *Bill Pryor/TG*

Above The station nameboard survives at the Exmoor
Museum in Lynton. *TG*

Lynton has an imposing Town Hall in Lee Road, which is still used for this purpose. The old photograph is obviously pre-1918 as there is no war memorial. There are still shops opposite the Town Hall, currently including an art studio and a printers, the latter selling excellent old photographs of the Lynton & Barnstaple Railway. The printer himself owns the old railway station. *Beaford Archive/TG*

The Trail picks up the South West Coast Path through the Valley of Rocks, past Lee Abbey (now a Christian conference and holiday centre) towards Woody Bay. The Lynton & Barnstaple Railway had a station named Woody Bay at the highest point on the line, but this was almost 2 miles inland at Martinhoe Cross, which is now on the A39 main road. At Woody Bay itself there is the remains of a pier, once part of a plan to develop the Bay as a tourist centre with arrival by steamer being one option and train another.

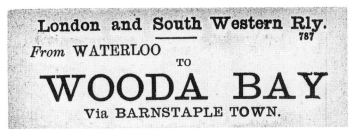

London and South Western Rly.
787
From WATERLOO
TO
WOODA BAY
Via BARNSTAPLE TOWN.

Author's collection

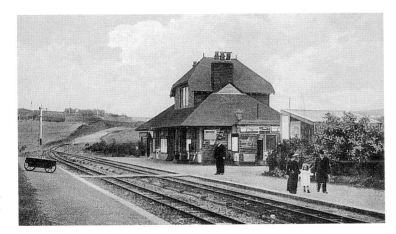

Woody Bay station, which was built by Mr R. Jones, is now privately owned and in most attractive surroundings. Both the hamlet and the station were formerly called Wooda Bay, the name changing in 1901. There are plans to restore a short section of the Lynton & Barnstaple Railway through the station. *Bill Pryor/TG*

Beyond Woody Bay the Coast Path continues to Heddon's Mouth and over Trentishoe and Holdstone Downs to the village of Combe Martin. Most of the area is designated of special scientific interest and is in the care of the National Trust. Continuing west the Coast Path approaches Ilfracombe over Hillsborough, which gives very good views of the harbour and the town beyond.

Ilfracombe railway station was located high above the town near Cairn Top. Many of the trains from London to Barnstaple ran on to Ilfracombe, which was the end of the line. The road seen in this old view of the town leads past the then new entrance to the station on the extreme left and continues round the base of the hill. A zigzag path from here takes one to Cairn Top, which gave an excellent view of the station.

The lorry (top left) is parked on the station approach road, now used for access to a factory built on the station site. The rear gardens of the houses nearest the camera in the 'past' view are now occupied by modern bungalows. The houses beyond the station approach still stand and many continue to offer bed and breakfast accommodation, despite closure of the railway. Houses also occupy the field on the right, where the merry-go-round can be seen. The Cairn is a Nature Reserve administered by Devon Wildlife Trust, and a visit to Cairn Top today finds the view obscured by trees; even in winter it is difficult to see the station site or the town. *Ilfracombe Museum/TG*

The station was rebuilt by the Southern Railway in 1928/9. Here the 'Atlantic Coast Express' waits to leave for Waterloo on 12 July 1957 behind 'Battle of Britain' Class No 34060 *25 Squadron*.

As the number of rail passengers declined, the trains became shorter and were eventually formed of single or two-car diesel multiple units, which were dwarfed beside the long island platform. This is the station in 1968, still open but already looking abandoned. *Frank Hornby/TG*

The Tarka Trail continues to use the South West Coast Path from Ilfracombe to Woolacombe, with its famous stretch of sandy beach, then to Croyde Bay and Braunton Burrows, before meeting the railway again. Apart from the section between Woolacombe and Putsborough, the Coast Path is unsuitable for cyclists and an alternative is to take the course of the railway from behind the site of Ilfracombe station, which is a designated cycle and footpath. This takes one almost as far as the next station up the line, namely Mortehoe & Woolacombe. 'Up' is a most appropriate term, as the line climbs at a gradient of 1 in 36 almost all the way and is thus marginally steeper than the line connecting Exeter Central and St David's.

The railway was cut out of the side of the hill and passes above the Slade Valley. The road through Slade village leads from Ilfracombe to Mortehoe & Woolacombe station. The cycle track stops at Lee Bridge, a little short of the site of this station, from which point the road can be used to reach Woolacombe village and the Tarka Trail proper. There is also a permissive footpath from Lee Bridge which uses the railway as far as the site of Morte Bridge.

The view from the train in 1957 with Slade village lying to the left. Ilfracombe engine shed and station awning are just visible in the distance.

The old railway line forms part of the Nature Reserve and passes through the up line tunnel and past two reservoirs in the valley below. The industrial building and chimney in the present-day view mark the site of Ilfracombe station. *Frank Hornby/TG*

Mortehoe & Woolacombe station in 1968, shortly after the up line had been removed as part of economies, which in the event were insufficient to prevent the line from closing. Morte Bridge is immediately beyond, and adjacent to the station is the 'Fortescue Arms'.

Remarkable events began to take place at the station in 1985. The buildings had been in private ownership for some years, but the platforms were abandoned and the track had been taken up. New track and several coaches appeared, as if a long deferred reinstatement of services was about to become a reality. But the reality was that this once country station was to become a children's playground.

This was opened in 1987, with an entrance fee far in excess of the cost of a platform ticket! By 1994, when this photograph was taken, the shallow cutting beyond the station had been filled in and Morte Bridge had been removed as part of a scheme to realign the road junction. The field to the right is used on summer weekends for an open air market and car boot sale - the ultimate desecration of the countryside! There is now a heritage centre in Mortehoe village, which is worth a visit. *All TG*

South of Mortehoe & Woolacombe the railway line descended sharply (1 in 40) all the way to Braunton, following the main Ilfracombe to Barnstaple road (the A361). The railway was built long before this road, and in Victorian times the road between Barnstaple and Ilfracombe was what is now the B3230 through Muddiford, more direct but much hillier.

The station in Braunton was situated where the road to Croyde crossed the railway. In this photograph, taken in the early 1920s and looking towards Ilfracombe, the level crossing can be seen between the two engines. It was here that, in steam days, additional engines were attached to heavy trains to give assistance on the long climb to Mortehoe.

Very little survives to link these two pictures. The level crossing was where the pedestrian crossing is now located, in the centre of the picture. *R. L. Knight/TG*

This view of the station in 1968 shows that there have been no major structural changes, although a house has been built on the Croyde side of the level crossing. The station is electrically lit, but still guarded by traditional semaphore signals and still providing the same basic seating.

The railway site is now occupied by a Countryside Centre, Health Centre, car park and youth club, the latter being housed in the old goods shed. Only this and the station house, which is now a newsagent, remain. The old-style van glimpsed through the bushes may lead one to assume that this too is an old photograph, but modern telephone boxes confirm that it is the present day. *Both TG*

The town centre is only a few yards to the east of the station and is at the intersection of the Croyde and Ilfracombe roads. A bus from Ilfracombe passes through the village in the early 1930s.

Although basically unchanged, the motor cars, proliferation of road markings, telegraph poles and general clutter all spoil what was a pleasant location. *R. L. Knight/TG*

The Tarka Trail approaches Braunton by way of Braunton Burrows, then along the west bank of the River Caen to join the railway line at what was the level crossing at Velator, about half a mile south of Braunton station. From here the Trail is suitable for cycling and uses the railway trackbed all the way to Barnstaple. The only station on this section is Wrafton.

Southern Railway.

5/23   787

TO

WRAFTON

Author's collection

Wrafton station looking towards Ilfracombe, taken during singling of the line in 1967.

The station buildings are now in use as a private house and several railway items have been retained, including the nameboard, platform electric lights and one of the signals (left). *Both TG*

The village of Wrafton is close by and this is the Post Office and general stores on the Barnstaple to Ilfracombe road in the 1920s.

A new main road was later built between this part of the village and the station, and the old route is now only a local road serving recently built houses. The Post Office still exists, however, even to the letter box in the wall.
R. L. Knight/TG

The old Chivenor Airfield, looking across the River Taw towards Barnstaple.

Today Chivenor is also used by the RAF Search and Rescue Helicopter Unit, which was established in 1958. This 1994 photograph was taken from the Tarka Trail. *R. L. Knight/TG*

Shortly after passing Wrafton railway station is Chivenor. An airfield was established here in 1934 to provide passenger and postal services to Lundy Island, South Wales and the South West. The airfield was taken over by the Royal Air Force at the beginning of the Second World War and was used as a fighter pilot training base, except between 1974 and 1980 when it was closed. That function ceased in 1995, and the base is now used by the Royal Marines.

From Chivenor to Barnstaple the railway, today the Tarka Trail, keeps to the north bank of the River Taw and gives good views of the opposite bank including Fremington Quay (see page 30). The Trail passes historic Heanton Court, which is now a pub; the next point of interest is Ashford lime kiln, which was restored in 1986 after falling into disuse at the beginning of the century.

The approach to Barnstaple is past the Pottington Industrial Estate. The Trail leaves the railway once it reaches the site of Pottington level crossing by the grounds of the Rugby Football Club. The railway crossed the River Yeo by a swing bridge which gave access to Rolle Quay and Pilton Wharf, but the bridge has been demolished, requiring a detour round the Quay itself; it is, however, planned to reinstate the swing bridge, and it is worth continuing along the railway to the point where the swing bridge was situated, before retracing one's steps to Pottington level crossing to take up the Trail.

The Trail runs alongside Rolle Quay, crosses the Rolle Bridge (the A361 Ilfracombe road), then along the south bank of the river to regain the railway between the Civic Centre and Barnstaple Town station.

The Town station was built on this site in 1898 and had a platform for the Barnstaple Junction and Ilfracombe trains and a bay from which the Lynton & Barnstaple Railway narrow-gauge trains began their journey. *Bill Pryor*

Even in 1968 the site of the bay for Lynton was readily discernable. The diesel multiple unit is working the 17.18 Exeter Central to Ilfracombe service on 27 July. The iron railway bridge and road bridge behind can be seen in the right background, while the town centre and cattle market lie to the left behind the houses. The modern library and North Devon Record Office are also nearby. *Ronald Lumber*

The present-day station site combines private flats, a restaurant and public walkway. The signal box at the far end of the station site is used by the Lynton & Barnstaple Railway Association, one of the main aims of which is to rebuild a section of the line, and much railway material has been collected in pursuit of this. *TG*

A few yards beyond the signal box is the site of the earlier LSWR Town station, on which a bus station was built in 1922. Railway signals can be seen behind the bus station building in this view from the mid-1920s.

This location, The Strand, is readily recognisable today and is still the bus station. The intervening period saw the growth of bus transport, and services were provided by larger and larger double-deck buses wherever they were not precluded by the narrow country roads. The last decade has, however, seen a shrinkage in the use of

buses, and almost all services are currently operated by one-man minibuses. Although the cafe in the foreground is now a discotheque, the building still appears to have the same cast iron drainpipes as those seen in the 'past' photograph. Note the contrasting lamp posts in the present-day photograph. The Queen Anne's Building in the background is scheduled to be converted into a heritage centre under the auspices of the Town Council. *R. L. Knight/TG*

The Strand brings the traveller to the museum by the Taw Bridge, and, by crossing the bridge, back to Barnstaple Junction Station.

THE TARKA TRAIL: SOUTH-WESTERN SECTION

The line from Barnstaple to Fremington was opened in 1848 and wagons were horse-drawn. It was converted to broad gauge in 1854 to connect with the new line from Crediton. It subsequently became part of the LSWR line through to Torrington, following the south bank of the River Taw to Instow where the Taw and Torridge flow into Bideford Bay. This part of the Trail is almost completely flat, but the cyclist in particular should not be lulled into thinking that the ride in one direction will be as easy on the return - the wind can be very strong along this section.

The approach to the first station of Fremington is through a shallow cutting, which opens out to reveal what was once a quay. This was built by the Taw Vale Railway & Dock Company and was used to import coal and export clay from the area around Petersmarland, south of Bideford. This is the station in 1967 when the line and quay were both operational.

The quay ceased to be used for rail-borne traffic in 1970 and subsequently fell into disuse, although it is soon due for regeneration with a heritage centre, etc. The station was also eventually demolished, and left in the state shown here until the area was prepared for the Tarka Trail. Adjacent to the station was an abattoir built in the 1950s, since closed and demolished in the early 1990s. *Both TG*

The railway next crosses a small creek known as the Pill, and from here a good overall view of the quayside and the adjacent station and sidings could be obtained. The iron bridge was built in 1880 to replace a wooden swing bridge.
    The same view today shows the popularity of the Trail. The footpath to the right leads to Fremington village and the Tarka Trail continues along the trackbed of the railway. To the left is Fremington lime kiln. *R. L. Knight/TG*

The line continues west and runs perfectly straight until it reaches East Yelland. There was no railway station here, but in the 1950s, amidst much local controversy, a power station complete with a jetty for deliveries of coal was built between the railway and the river bank. Sidings were included and brought some revenue to the railway. It was officially opened on 21 April 1955 by Earl Fortescue, but had a life of less than 40 years before being decommissioned in 1984. There followed more controversy over its fate, and it was eventually demolished.

The land is now derelict and inaccessible due to contamination, but the contaminated land is shortly to be capped over and there is a proposal to re-open the jetty for commercial shipping. The only building remaining is the one on the far left of the 'past' photograph, seen here from a slightly different angle. This is one of the least attractive sights along the Tarka Trail, and is a demonstration of man's insensitivity. There is a footpath round the perimeter of the power station site that passes the jetty, and this can be used by walkers as an alternative to the railway line. *Cyril Found/TG*

River and railway line turn south-west for the approach to Instow. After passing the Royal Marines Amphibious Trials and Training Unit, the railway ran behind the village in a shallow cutting. This is the 1 pm from Waterloo to Torrington on 30 June 1958. The Class 'M7' tank engine, No 30252, was attached at Barnstaple, the greater part of the train continuing to Ilfracombe behind a more substantial engine. The same location today shows an unusually deserted Tarka Trail. *Both TG*

On the opposite bank of the River Torridge is Appledore, and a ferry operates between there and Instow. The jetty at Instow is a good place from which to see the row of houses and shops at the south end of the village. In the distance is the railway level crossing, signal box and station, seen in the 1920s.

This almost identical photograph may give rise to confusion. The signal box still stands, suggesting that the railway is still in operation, yet the fare on the ferry is in decimal currency. The photograph was in fact taken in 1993, and Instow signal box, which is a Grade II listed building, has been preserved as a reminder of the former presence of the railway. It is open to visitors on Sundays during the summer, under the care of the Bideford & Instow Railway Group. *R. L. Knight/TG*

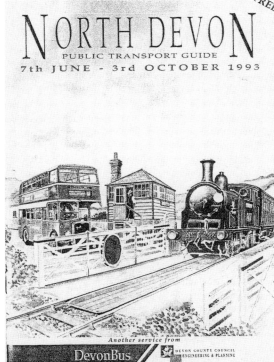

NORTH DEVON
PUBLIC TRANSPORT GUIDE
7th JUNE - 3rd OCTOBER 1993

Another service from

DevonBus   DEVON COUNTY COUNCIL
ENGINEERING & PLANNING

ENQUIRIES: EXETER BARNSTAPLE OR PLYMOUTH 382800

Above Instow station was on a curve, with the main building on the river side. This is the view looking toward Barnstaple in 1967.

In addition to the signal box, the Torrington-bound platform still exists in a good state of repair, together with traditional railway-style railings. On the left are the premises of the North Devon Yacht Club, which owns the main station building, little changed from railway days apart from the loss of the awning. *Both TG*

Above right The most attractive front cover of the North Devon Public Transport Guide for the summer of 1993 shows both bus and train at Instow. *Reproduced courtesy of Devon County Council, Environment Department*

Right In BR days the station was electrically lit using lamps of an unusual design attached to the old LSWR cast iron posts. *TG*

Departure from Instow on 30 June 1958 finds Class 'M7' No 30254 hauling a set of Southern Railway main-line coaches. The train had left Exeter at 4.21 pm and was due to arrive at Torrington at 6.24 pm. Today yachts dominate the scene; the Tarka Trail runs immediately behind the yachts on the right. *Both TG*

When the railway was first built, the terminus for Bideford was at Cross Parks. This later became the goods yard and the railway itself was extended to Torrington in 1872 with a new Bideford station on an embankment above the eastern end of the road bridge over the River Torridge. In this early view, probably dating from the 1940s, the town of Bideford lies across the river.

The goods yard was closed in 1965 and the land is now occupied by private houses built about 13 years ago. The area lay derelict for many years and some of the old quayside buildings towards the bridge still stand. The premises of I. Baker & Son (General Building Material and Coal Merchants) can be seen from Bideford station. *R. L. Knight/TG*

The new station was built in a cramped position and was flanked on one side by the Royal Hotel and on the other by a row of houses in Springfield Terrace. The road approach was under a low bridge then immediately up a steep hill on a sharp bend. This is the view looking toward Barnstaple in 1951 with Class 'M7' No 30255 on a Torrington train.

In common with other stations on the Tarka Trail, the loop was later taken out as an economy measure, as seen in the second view, dating from the late 1970s. The remaining track was lifted in 1984.

All that was said above about the approach to the station still applies today. The main buildings and platforms still stand and are in excellent repair. A signal box has been reconstructed on the platform, and there is track through the station with signals at each end and rolling-stock in the platform.

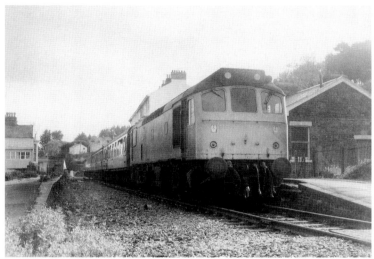

The restoration of the station is mainly the work of the Bideford & Instow Railway Group with support from the local authority and numerous other bodies. The Group was formed in 1988 to recreate as far as possible the railway atmosphere at Bideford and Instow railway stations, and this they have already achieved, although no doubt a lot more will be done in the future. The signal box houses the Group's museum which is open to the public on Sunday afternoons from Easter to October. The main station building is owned by Devon County Council and the coach (BR Mark I No 4489, delivered in 1992 from the Mid Hants Railway) is used by the Devon Countryside Service for a natural history display and tea room. Further items of rolling-stock have since been added.

It is most unfortunate that the plans to keep the line open with funding from the European Commission did not materialise. But then perhaps there would have been no new road bridge over the River Torridge and no Tarka Trail, both of which are generally regarded as positive developments. *Lens of Sutton/Alan Wilkinson/TG*

Author's collection

Southern Railway.

7/23   787

TO

BIDEFORD

Above A typical station scene from the 1920s, before the advent of milk tank wagons in the 1940s - except that this photograph was taken at Bideford in 1993. *TG*

Below left Somewhat older notices can also be inspected, such as this warning about the dangers of nakedness. *TG*

Below Bideford station is 220½ miles from Waterloo, as indicated on this old plate, which can still be seen by the side of the Tarka Trail. *TG*

L.&.S.W.R.
NEITHER MATCHES
NOR LIGHTS MUST
BE TAKEN NEAR
STORED PARAFFIN

20½ MILES
FROM WATERLOO
STATION LONDON.

There was another railway at Bideford, and this was the Bideford, Westward Ho! & Appledore Railway, which ran from the town quay to the other places in its title. It was opened in 1901 and ran along the road parallel to the quay, seen here, to Victoria Park where it turned west toward Westward Ho!. It was only 7 miles long and had 13 stations and halts. The railway closed in 1917 and the stock was requisitioned by the Government.

Since the 'past' photograph was taken, the Quay House has acquired a dome and other modifications, the trees have matured and all the attributes of modern society, such as the car park and road markings, are apparent. There is a booking office on the quay from where tickets for Lundy Island can be purchased.
Beaford Archive/TG

The most attractive (and hilly) part of the Trail accessible to cyclists begins at Bideford, and for those visitors short of time, this is the section for which to aim.

The first major landmark beyond Bideford is an iron bridge that takes the railway over the River Torridge near Landcross. On 22 March 1982 Class '31' No 31286 hauls a train of wagons containing ball clay from Marland to Barnstaple.

The view is easy to locate today, as it is from the main Torrington to Bideford (A386) road. It is fortunate that this and the other bridges over the Torridge were not demolished following closure of the line, as all are now used for the Tarka Trail. Cyclists are visible on the bridge in this 1994 view. Beyond Landcross the railway used part of the old canal route.
David Mitchell/TG

Road and railway continue to run parallel until the outskirts of Torrington, at times climbing steeply. After passing through a short tunnel under the main road, Weare Giffard can be seen on the opposite bank, a picturesque village most of which straddles a minor road also leading to Torrington.

This old photograph taken adjacent to the railway line shows the village school and quayside cottages. Weare Giffard is the ancestral home of the Fortescue family.

   Those buildings can now be seen from the Tarka Trail through gaps in the trees on the embankment, which are being managed in blocks to enable 'snapshot' views. Glimpses of the village can also be had at river level, but this is all that was visible in the spring of 1994, with the old school house still standing. *Beaford Archive/TG*

A short distance further on the railway crosses the river again; a parallel bridge, from where these photographs were taken, carried the Rolle Canal over the River Torridge. It was near here that Tarka the Otter was born and where he was last seen in a fight to the death with a hound. The canal, built by Lord Rolle in 1823, connected the Town Mills with the navigable part of the River Torridge between Weare Giffard and Landcross. It closed in 1871 and the aqueduct is now used to carry a private road into Beam House Activity Centre. On 25 June 1978 Class '33' No 33103 crosses the river with a special passenger train to Torrington. Cyclists and walkers occupy the same position in the 1994 view. *David Mitchell/TG*

The final approach to Torrington station is level, and this close-up view in 1956 shows Class 'M7' No 30247 with through coaches to Waterloo that will form the 'Atlantic Coast Express'.

In 1994 the end of the platform was completely overgrown, with the station buildings and road bridge only just visible. The platform has since been cleared of vegetation and reinstated with bike racks and seats, while the station building is now a public house. *Both TG*

On 23 April 1963 Class '2MT' No 41297 is ready to take just one coach on to Halwill Junction. The main-line coaches on the left are bound for Waterloo.

The same location after the cessation of passenger services shows the station building to be still in good repair, as if waiting to take on another role. Milk trains continued to run from here until 1978, and fertiliser was brought by rail until 1980. The last train from Torrington was a special passenger train, which ran in January 1983. *Terry Nicholls/TG*

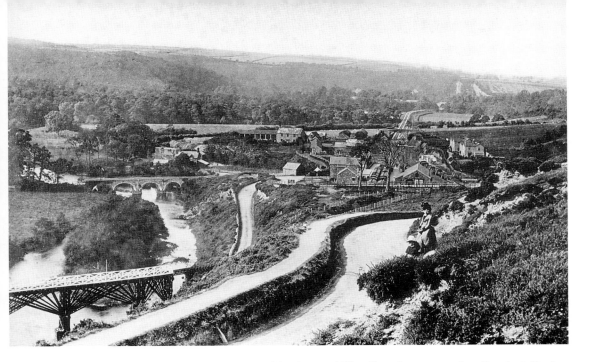

Rail passengers arriving at Torrington were faced with a long uphill walk to the town, unless they took the bus or one of the taxis that met all major trains. This Victorian era photograph from the hill shows the station in the middle distance and the line stretching toward Barnstaple. In the left foreground is the wooden bridge carrying the narrow-gauge mineral line, which was opened in 1881, to the Marland ball clay works. Clay was transferred to standard-gauge wagons at Torrington and taken to Bideford or Fremington for shipping, or continued by rail to various destinations in mainland Britain.

The view from this location today is rather different, as the road is no longer visible and there are many more trees. The roof of the station, the cottages to the right and the trackbed confirm that this is the same spot. *Beaford Archive/TG*

The nearest village to Torrington station was Taddiport, and this turn-of-the-century photograph shows the village, looking north-east. This was at one time the only route by road to Hatherleigh and Okehampton, but the main road now runs through Torrington town and crosses the River Torridge at Town Mills near the Royal Horticultural Society's Rosemoor Gardens; it was at Town Mills that several otter hunts used to gather. The mineral line lay some distance behind the camera, having swung west to follow the valley of a tributary of the River Torridge. The Torridge itself is in the foreground.

The cottages still exist today and the village is little changed. A major contributor to the economy of the village, and indeed the surrounding area, was the dairy factory, which opened in 1874. This also provided regular traffic for the railway, particularly milk for the Home Counties. In later years the milk traffic was all transferred to road, and the factory ultimately became a creamery under Dairy Crest, but this was closed in 1993. *Beaford Archive/TG*

Torrington town is located on some of the highest ground in the area and is well worth a visit. There are excellent views of the surrounding countryside and numerous walks over Torrington Common. Part of the Rolle Canal is a footpath. Fortunately the decline of the local dairy industry has to some extent been compensated by the building in 1967 of a glass factory, where the world famous Dartington Crystal is produced.

Above is an early photograph of the main road (New Street) through Torrington looking towards Bideford, with the Royal Exchange on the right. The road has been upgraded to form the A386 to Hatherleigh and Okehampton.
Beaford Archive/TG

The narrow-gauge mineral line was replaced in 1925 by a standard-gauge line connected directly to the existing terminus at Torrington. The location of the old mineral railway is clearly indicated at Torrington station, as there is a small arch under the road bridge adjacent to the standard-gauge arch used by the Trail. The new line, known as the North Devon & Cornwall Junction Light Railway, was worked by the Southern Railway from the outset and provided passenger as well as freight services. At its other end it connected with the ex-LSWR North Cornwall line at Halwill Junction, by that time also part of the Southern Railway network.

The bridge carrying the mineral railway was a major landmark that could be seen from the hill between Torrington town and station. The same viewpoint today shows the standard-gauge railway bridge in its new guise as part of the Tarka Trail. *Beaford Archive/TG*

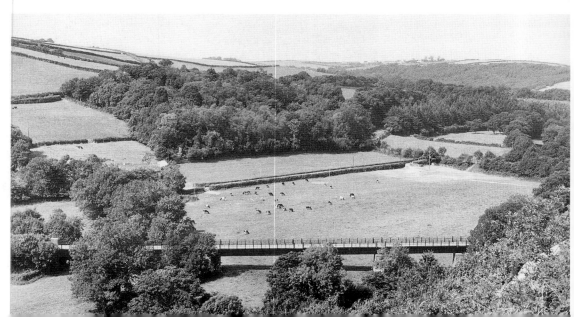

This vantage point gives superb views across the bridge. A mixed passenger and freight train approaches Torrington from Halwill Junction on 27 September 1962 behind Class '2MT' No 41238.

A wider perspective shows Class '31' No 31286 approaching Torrington on 22 March 1982 with a ball clay train from Marland. It was only six months later that the last clay train ran. The bridge now forms part of the Tarka Trail. *R. C. Riley/David Mitchell*

The new line followed the course of the narrow-gauge line for the first 6 miles. It was built to basic standards and provided several halts in isolated locations, the first of which beyond Torrington was Watergate (see back cover). The railway crossed an ungated road immediately beyond the halt, and on 6 October 1978 Class '25' No 25225 approaches the crossing with a train from Meeth and Marland clay works.

Today there are gates protecting users of the trackbed from the road, and preventing motorists from trying to drive along the Trail! *David Mitchell/TG*

The railway continues to climb almost until Yarde Halt is reached, the steepest part being 1 in 45. Yarde served adjacent clay workers' cottages and here also the railway was intersected by a minor road. Long before the advent of the railway, this was the main road from Taddiport to Hatherleigh, and it did not lose this status until construction of a new road (now the A386) between the Gribble Inn and Friars Hele via Meeth.

The cottages and platform are still there and on the opposite side of the road is a small car park for those wishing to leave their vehicles and take the Trail. *R. C. Riley/TG*

The line descends steeply to Dunsbear Halt, and thereafter gradients are a little more gentle. Dunsbear Halt was used by men employed at the nearby works of the North Devon Clay Company, which was connected to the 'main' line by a siding a few yards south of the Halt. This view, taken in September 1956, shows a mixed train bound for Torrington.

Passenger services between Torrington and Halwill Junction were withdrawn in 1965, but today remnants of the platform are still visible, as is the course of the line. The Halt is used as a resting place for walkers and cyclists, although self-sufficiency in refreshments is essential. The foreground was once occupied by a short siding. *H. C. Casserley/TG*

The sidings within the clay works were extensive and this early view shows the effective use of mechanisation, albeit rather crude. The works' narrow-gauge railway ceased to operate in 1970, and by contrast the present-day view shows the modern automated plant. *Beaford Archive/TG*

Petrockstowe was a more substantial station with a passing loop and two platforms. There was an early morning train from Torrington that ran only as far as here, returning to Torrington after a pause of nearly an hour. There was also a late afternoon train that started from Petrockstowe, but there was no balancing public service bringing the train from Torrington. Timings were very generous at all halts and stations to allow for shunting if the train was mixed. Torrington to Halwill Junction was 20¹/₂ miles, and the scheduled journey time was 1¹/₂ hours. In the first view, taken in the late 1950s, the afternoon Torrington train whittles away the time at Petrockstowe.

Today both platforms still exist, but all railway buildings except a platelayers' hut have gone. *Chris Gammell/TG*

The village of Petrockstowe is about a mile away and it is obvious from its size that the railway could never have realistically expected to have generated much passenger revenue. This is the main street in the 1900s and little is different today, except that the shop has become a private house and telegraph and electric cables intrude. This was the Taddiport to Hatherleigh road; after the building of the new road through Meeth (see page 53), Petrockstowe ceased to be a port of call for through traffic. *Beaford Archive/TG*

The Trail continues along the old railway line, with a short detour around the clay pits, to Meeth Halt. This was the only place where the line crossed a main road (A386). A few years ago there was a clear view of the road from the Torrington end of the platform, and despite having been closed for two years when this visit was made in 1967, no one had seen fit to remove the station nameboard. Beyond Meeth the line closed completely when passenger services were withdrawn between Torrington and Halwill Junction in 1965, and the track was lifted the following year.

The halt is still in existence, but since this photograph was taken it has been totally reinstated, the platform cleared, the nameboard replaced and the buildings renovated and re-roofed. *Both TG*

The village of Meeth is close by and these two photographs taken about 70 years apart show remarkably little change - the cottage has been extended and this is now the Post Office. A visit to the Bull and Dragon public house (to the right of the photograph) is well worth while, and excellent food is served. *Beaford Archive/TG*

Opposite This is Bridge Street, Hatherleigh (the main road), in the 1920s looking toward Torrington. Locating this point proved quite difficult in 1994, as the road junction has been changed and the corner shop of Messrs Beaven had been demolished in the 1960s to reveal the thatched cottages behind. The bakery advertising Hovis still stands, however, and this was the first clue, although it is now a private house. Some of the cottages on the left have been demolished and a new Town Hall built. On the left the steep-gabled building confirms the location. *Beaford Archive/TG*

This page Hatherleigh station was inconveniently situated north-west of the town; reaching it involved first a steep climb along the main road, then a long descent down a country lane. Both the town and the station are on the River Lew, which flows into the Torridge just north of the station. This view of the station in the early 1960s shows Class '2MT' No 41298 on a ball clay train for Halwill Junction. By this time the original wooden post signals had been replaced by rail-built posts.

A close-up of the Halwill end of the station during a visit two years after closure found most of the ironmongery still in place. The bridge in the background brings the country lane from Hatherleigh past the station approach road (see overleaf) It is hoped eventually to extend the cycleway section of the Trail from Meeth to Hatherleigh along the railway where possible. *Lens of Sutton/TG*

This photograph, taken from almost under the lane bridge seen in the picture on the previous page, shows the approach road and was taken shortly after the line was opened and before the installation of water cranes.

Today the cutting between the station and bridge is completely overgrown, but the approach road is clear and forms the private access road to the former station buildings, which have been extended and are now a private residence. *Beaford Archive/TG*

The railway turns west beyond Hatherleigh to reach Halwill Junction, 7¾ miles away, but this is not part of the Tarka Trail. The Trail proper turns south-east and, using footpaths and country lanes, passes through Jacobstowe before reaching Okehampton. The Trail then picks up the River Taw, which it follows closely until it reaches the Tarka Line near Eggesford. This part of the Trail is covered in the companion book, *The Tarka and Dartmoor Lines*.

BIBLIOGRAPHY

Transport

Back Along the Lines, Victor Thompson (Badger Books, 1983) ISBN 0 946290 03 0
The Barnstaple and Ilfracombe Railway, Colin G. Maggs (Oakwood Press, 1988)
    ISBN 0 85361 368 0
The Bideford, Westward Ho! & Appledore Railway, Julia and Jonathan Baxter
    (H. J. Chard & Sons) ISBN 0 9507330 1 6
The Bideford, Westward Ho! & Appledore Railway, Stanley C. Jenkins (Oakwood Press, 1993)
    ISBN 0 85361 452 0
Branch Line to Lynton, Vic Mitchell and Keith Smith (Middleton Press, 1992) ISBN 1 873793 0 49
Branch Lines to Torrington, Vic Mitchell and Keith Smith (Middleton Press, 1994)
    ISBN 1 873793 37 5
Devon and Cornwall Railways in Old Photographs, Kevin Robertson (Alan Sutton, 1989)
    ISBN 0 86299 667 8
Lines to Torrington, John Nicholas (Oxford Publishing Company, 1984) ISBN 0 86093 145 5
The Lynton and Barnstaple Railway, L. T. Catchpole (Oakwood Press, 1988) ISBN 085361 363 X
The Lynton and Barnstaple Railway, G. A. Brown, J. D. C. Prideaux and H. G. Radcliffe
    (David & Charles, 1971)
The Lynton and Barnstaple Railway Album, J. D. C. A. Prideaux (David & Charles, 1974)
The North Devon and Cornwall Junction Light Railway, C. F. D. Whetmath and Douglas Stuckey
    (Forge Books, 1980)
Railway Landmarks in Devon, Jean Hall (David & Charles, 1982) ISBN 0 7153 8363 9
A Regional History of the Railways of Great Britain, Volume I: The West Country,
    David St John Thomas (David & Charles, 1981) ISBN 0 7153 8210 1
The Southern West of Salisbury, Terry Gough (Oxford Publishing Company, 1984)
    ISBN 0 86093 341 5
Take Off from Chivenor, Lois Lamplugh (Maslands Ltd, 1990) ISBN 0 946290 21 0
The Tarka and Dartmoor Lines: A Past and Present Companion, Terry Gough (Past & Present, 1998)
    ISBN 1 85895 139 9
Walking West Country Railways, Christopher Somerville (David & Charles, 1982)
    ISBN 0 7153 8143 1

Ordnance Survey Maps

First Edition (approx 1880): sheets 74, 82, reprinted by David & Charles, 1970
Popular Edition (approx 1918): sheets 118, 127, 128, 137
New Popular Edition (approx 1940): sheets 163, 175, 176
Landranger Series (current): sheets 180, 191

Town and Country

Barnstaple and North West Devon (Fifteenth Edition, Ward Lock, 1952)
Barnstaple, Town on the Taw, Lois Lamplugh (Phillimore, 1983)
Barnstaple Yesterday, Julia Barnes and Jonathan Baxter (Robert & Young, 1992)
Braunton, Tina Gaydon (Badger, 1989) ISBN 0946 29020 2
Changing Devon, James Derounian, Chris Smith and Chris Chapman (Tabb House Ltd, 1988)
Devon Town Trails, Peter Hunt and Marilyn Wills (Devon Books, 1988)
Exploring Barnstaple, John Bradbeer (Thematic Books, 1990) ISBN 0 948444 177
Exploring Bideford, Peter Christine (Thematic Books, 1989) ISBN 0 948444 169
Fremington Village and Pill, J. D. Collins, 1992
A History of Ilfracombe, Lois Lamplugh (Phillimore, 1984) ISBN 0 85033 525 6
Ilfracombe, A Pictoral Record, Glenn K. Horridge (Ammonite Books, 1986) ISBN 1 869866 00 2
Ilfracombe's Yesterdays, Lilian Wilson (Adrienne and Peter Oldale, 1976)
Instow Town and Old Yelland, J. D. Collins, 1992

The Lyn in Flood, Peter Keene and Derek Elsom (Thematic Books, 1990) ISBN 0948444 20 07
The Lynmouth Flood Disaster, Eric R. Delderfield (ERD, 1953) ISBN 0 900345 00 4
Market Towns of North Devon, Rosemary Anne Lauder (Badger Books, 1983) ISBN 0 946290 04 0
North Devon Country in Old Photographs (Parts I and II), Beryl Yates (Alan Sutton, 1989)
    ISBNs 0 86299 652X, 0 86299 727 5
North Devon Coast in Old Photographs, Beryl Yates (Alan Sutton, 1989) ISBN 0 86299 653 8
Picture Postcard Braunton, Bob Davis (Robert & Young, 1993) No ISBN
Postcard Views of North Devon, Volume I (Ilfracombe), Volume II (Barnstaple),
    Volume III (South Molton), Tom Bartlett (Badger Books)
A Tale of Two Rivers, Rosemary Anne Lauder (1985) ISBN 0 946 290 11 3
Tarka Country, Trevor Beer (Badger Books, 1983) ISBN 0 946 290 059
The Tarka Trail, A Walker's Guide, produced by the Tarka Project (Devon Books, 5th ed,1998)
    ISBN 0 86114 8770 0
Valley of the Rocks, Lynton, Peter Keene and Brian Pearce (Thematic Books, 1993)
    ISBN 0 948 444 25 8
Vanished Landmarks of North Devon, Rosemary Lauder (North Devon Books)
    ISBN 0 946 290 237
A Visitor's Guide to Devon, Brian Le Messurier (Moorland Publishing, 1983)
Woody Bay, Harriet Bridle (Merlin Books, 1991) ISBN 0 86303 510 8

Further information on Tarka Country and the Tarka Line is available from the Tarka Country Tourism Association, 01271 345008.

INDEX OF LOCATIONS

Barnstaple 9
    Taw bridges 10-11
    town 29
    Town station 28
    Victoria station 12
Beam Bridge 44
Bideford 38-40
    town 41
Braunton 23-23
    town 24

Chivenor 27

Dunsbear Halt 54
    clay works 55

East Yelland power station 32

Fremington 30
    quay 31

Hatherleigh 61-62
    town 60

Ilfracombe 18-20
Instow 33-37

Landcross bridge 42
Landkey 13
Lynton & Lynmouth 14-15
    Lynton Town Hall 16

Meeth Halt 58
    village 59

Mortehoe & Woolacombe 21

Petrockstowe 56
    village 57

Taddiport 48
Torrington 6, 45-47
    town 49
    viaduct near 50-51

Watergate Halt 52
Weare Giffard 43
Woody Bay 17
Wrafton 25
    village 26

Yarde Halt 53